Righteousness and Life from Grace

THE GOSPEL OF CHRIST IN ROMANS

RIGHTEOUSNESS AND LIFE FROM

Grace

JERRY SERIGHT

Pleasant Word
A Division of WinePress Group
PW

Initial cover sketch by Jose de Menezes.

Pleasant Word (a division of WinePress Publishing, PO Box 428, Enumclaw, WA 98022) functions only as book publisher. As such, the ultimate design, content, editorial accuracy, and views expressed or implied in this work are those of the author.

Unless otherwise noted, all Scriptures are taken from the *King James Version* of the Bible.

ISBN 13: 978-1-4141-1228-2
ISBN 10: 1-4141-1228-9
Library of Congress Catalog Card Number: 2008902959

To Mr. Wolfgang Bodeker, for his expert keyboarding of the text, and to Mr. Huneldo de Alencar, for his indispensable correction of the Portuguese—men whose absence in my life would have prevented not only the realization of this work, but also the birth of a lasting friendship.

To my dearest wife, Coleen, for her capitulation to this, my dream. May God reserve for her a place of honor in the great beyond.

To the Brazilian nation, whose kindness and love are beyond comparison.

Contents

"Therefore as by the offence of one, Judgment came upon all men to condemnation: even so by the righteousness of one the free gift came upon all men unto justification of life."

—Romans 5:18

Preface

*O*N MY ENDEAVOR to present the Gospel completely—telling the story from beginning to end—I stumbled onto the epistle of Paul to the Romans. I discovered in the sixteen chapters of Romans a dramatic presentation of the Gospel that tells the whole story, beginning with the state of man before Christ, going on to show the grace God made available to man, and finally, giving witness of the reconciliation between God and man. What's more, I "uncovered" this same whole story in the epistle's first six chapters! The whole story of the Roman Christians (or saints) is there, as well as your story and mine. And this personal identification with the story has proven to be a greater discovery even than finding the whole Gospel in Romans!

My new encounter with Romans stimulated me to re-read my Bible from beginning to end. In the following four years, I read it three times—twice in English and once in Portuguese. (Nearly all of the first sixteen years of my life were spent in Brazil.) And each reading of the Bible heightened my appreciation of Romans. All the principal points in the Bible's redemptive story—the human condition, God's desire and effort to redeem humanity, and His grace in providing this redemption in Christ—can be found in Romans. On occasions, I have used Romans exclusively to teach the Gospel. When I served as a missionary in Brazil from October 2000 to September 2001 and the opportunity presented itself for a newspaper study in a major northeast Brazil newspaper, Romans was my book of choice. *Righteousness and Life from Grace* is a product of that newspaper study—and of my discovery of the Gospel in the epistle to the Romans.

But there is more to the appeal of Romans than its practical teaching. The epistle's dramatic presentation of God's "story" is unsurpassed in the New Testament, and the drama's narrator, the apostle Paul, is at his best! With his vivid descriptions of mankind living in the world of sin, and his citations from the Old Testament—introduced directly into the drama of Romans—you will feel like you are there, witnessing all of that! For instance, in Romans 2 when Paul constructs the scene of the good man who lives by the law, he borrows a line from the Psalms to show us mankind's impossible plight before God, who, according to Paul's citation, "Will render to every man according to his deeds" (Rom. 2:6–7; cf. Ps. 62:12).

In the epistle's following chapter, Paul takes us even deeper into the valley of the human condition, with still another quotation from the Psalms: "There is none righteous, no, not even one" (Rom. 3:10; cf. Ps. 14:1–3). He doesn't leave us in that valley, but to find your way out, you're going to have to "attend" the drama. The preceding lines are from the drama's opening scene (Rom. 1:18–3:20), which I have entitled, "From Where We Came: the World of Sin." (But this is a drama with a good ending—following this opening scene, Paul turns his drama decidedly upward!)

In *Righteousness and Life from Grace*, I have striven not to rob the reader of the satisfaction Paul's epistle to the Romans has afforded me, because I want you to read Romans. For this reason, I have included the text of the first six chapters of Romans, so you can see, for yourself, Paul's dramatic presentation of the Gospel. The primary initiative I intend to foster with the writing of this book is the reading of the sacred Scriptures. Thus, in order for the text of Romans to receive its rightful preeminence in Paul's drama, I have kept each grouping of verses as minimally separated as possible from the next block of text, all in the hope that my discussion of the text won't unnecessarily interrupt the apostle's logic, nor the beauty of what was written. Economy of words was my most sacred rule. I don't want to tire the reader. If you are able to read the book in two or three hours, then good! If, after a while, you begin a second reading, then very good!

I don't hide the fact that I have affection for the Brazilian people. Conversations I had about Romans with this or that person provided much of the motivation for the carrying out of this project. My mere presence in Brazil, with all its reminders of the necessity of God's grace over the Brazilian people, sufficed for motivation. I remember, for instance, a particular conversation with an Internal Revenue employee, who, when he orally had read me the first chapter of Romans, commented, "There are so many people in Brazil who are excluded." (He said this in reference to the Brazilian Indians, the extremely poor, etc.) I recalled this, early in my writing, when I reached Romans 1:5–6: "By whom we have received grace and apostleship, for obedience to the faith among all nations, for his name: Among whom are ye also the called of Jesus Christ …" The Gospel is for all.

But the greatest motivation to see the job through came from the significance Romans adds to my own story. More than once at the end of an intense struggle to reproduce the meaning of a particular text (usually late at night), I would reflect, *Is what I have in Christ really that good? Or He really did all that—to that degree of perfection?* (At times, I even cried.) If in a place in this book (or two!) you find my emotions caused me to detour, then pardon. If you look closer, you will find, here and there, the apostle doing the same. It is simply the normal reaction of a person who has experienced God's righteousness and life—by His grace!

I recommend to you the epistle of Paul to the Romans. In it, you will find the proclamation of the Gospel (1:16–17). In its first six chapters, you will find enough of the story of justification in Christ to have the beginning and end. There you also will find the story of the Roman Christians. Finally, you will find your own story—at some point you will find yourself in these six chapters. From then on, the apostle will be telling the story to you!

I also offer for your consideration the reading of *Righteousness and Life from Grace*. It is my desire that the Gospel be more available to people. I hope that, if nothing else, at least the attention given to Romans will place the Gospel in the hands of the people. The Gospel is a story, beautiful and compelling. My search for a way to tell it in all its majesty and appeal led me to the opening of Romans: The whole story, in order, with nothing missing—in six chapters! Read the whole story, then read the rest of Romans, and then read the rest of the Book: "For whatsoever things were written aforetime were written for our learning, that we through patience and comfort of the scriptures might have hope" (Rom. 15:4).

CHAPTER 1

The Life Within Our Reach
(1:1–17)

THE STORY OF the Roman Christians (in chapters 1 through 6) starts at the end—that is, at the time of their receiving this epistle—and then works its way back to the beginning, from where they had come (see 6:19–22 for an illustration of this). After introducing himself and his Gospel in verses 1 through 17, Paul immediately plunges into an eternal drama: the boundless story of humanity, from its inception, to its fusion with the story of Christ, the story of the Roman Christians, and the story of you and me.

The contents of Paul's epistle to the Romans give us a diary—a type of historical portfolio of the lives of these Roman Christians. A great many of them had a Gentile background (Rom. 15:15–18; 1:5–6). Others had a Jewish upbringing (Rom. 2:17–29). Paul narrates this Jewish and Gentile drama altogether too realistically. Its presence will draw you in quickly, and you soon will begin to interest yourself in the players in Paul's drama.

At some point in the drama, your affinity for the players will turn into identity with the players: "My story is being

1

told!" you will discover. "And it is really how he is telling it!" That's because this story is the Gospel, and the one telling it is God. And everybody—Paul, Christ, the Romans, and you and I—are in this story.

But I'm getting just a little bit ahead of myself. Paul first addresses the Roman Christians in the present and "visits" with them a bit (1:1–17), and then he proclaims to the whole world the story given him (1:1) about all of us, from beginning to end! After he replays the Roman Christians' history (in chapters 1 through 6), and works his way back to the updated, full-grown Romans (in chapter 6), Paul briefly revisits where they had come from (6:19–22). Let us look, then, in chapter 1 (vv. 1–17), to these new, Gospel-raised Romans to see "The Life Within Our Reach."

Full Membership in the Spiritual Family of God (1:1–7)

1 Paul, a servant of Jesus Christ, called to be an apostle, separated unto the gospel of God,

2 (which he had promised afore by his prophets in the Holy Scriptures,)

3 Concerning his Son Jesus Christ our Lord, which was made of the seed of David according to the flesh;

4 And declared to be the Son of God with power, according to the spirit of holiness, by the resurrection from the dead:

5 By whom we have received grace and apostleship, for obedience to the faith among all nations, for his name:

6 Among whom are ye also the called of Jesus Christ:

7 To all that be in Rome, beloved of God, called to be saints: Grace to you and peace from God our Father, and the Lord Jesus Christ.

Paul's first order of business is to establish the authoritative source of his epistle (vv.1–3): "The Gospel of God... concerning his Son Jesus Christ our Lord." (We will see directly that it is concerning all of us as well.) The Gospel is the vessel from which Paul will draw out the contents of his epistle. The parenthetical phrase in verse 2 gives the reach of the Gospel: "which he had promised afore by his prophets in the Holy Scriptures" (in this case, the Old Testament). Verses 3 and 4 give the content of the Gospel—"concerning his Son Jesus Christ"—and verse 5, the wonderful product of the Gospel: "By whom we have received grace," further abbreviating our previously-declared, complete Gospel story from six chapters all the way down to five verses! If a single verse were to be decided upon as being the most telling of Christ's utter essentiality in our salvation, verse 5 would have to be in the running: "By whom we have received grace." The whole epistle to the Romans is a declaration of how, through Christ, God funneled His grace to man.

The Romans—and the Apostle Paul—had been "called of Jesus Christ" and "called to be saints" (vv. 6–7). This appeals to us for several reasons: 1) The idea of inclusion—we who, in varying measure, are acquainted with exclusion; 2) The idea of importance—the Romans had not been overlooked; 3) The idea of belonging, which is indispensable. The expression that most reflects the apostle's exuberance in belonging and being a servant of Jesus Christ is found in verse 3: "Jesus Christ our Lord!" Jesus Christ is the principal figure in this salutation (vv. 1–17), as well as in the entire epistle. The epistle to the Romans presents us not with a "system," but with a man: "Jesus Christ...declared to be the Son of God with power... by the resurrection from the dead." The Roman saints had been called to be of this One!

3

Glossary

Apostle: "1. A delegate, messenger, one sent forth with orders. 2. Especially applied to the twelve disciples whom Christ selected out of the multitude of his adherents, to be his constant companions and the heralds to proclaim to men the kingdom of God. With these apostles Paul claimed equality, because through a heavenly intervention he had been appointed by the ascended Christ himself to preach the gospel among the Gentiles and owed his knowledge of the way of salvation not to man's instruction but to direct revelation from Christ himself, and moreover had evidenced his apostolic qualifications by many signal proofs (Gal. 1:1, 11–12)."[1]

Gospel: "In the N.T. (New Testament), the term is applied to the revelation of God's plan for reconciling man to Himself by forgiving his sin and by transforming his character."[2]

Grace: "Free favour, specially manifested by God towards man in the Gospel scheme."[3]

Faith: "Used especially of the faith by which a man embraces Jesus, i.e., a conviction, full of joyful trust, that Jesus is the Messiah—the divinely appointed author of eternal salvation in the Kingdom."[4]

Nations: In Romans, "all who are not Jews," that is, the rest of the world; *Gentiles* is a synonymous term. W.J. Conybeare's observation regarding God's promise to Abraham—"I have made thee the father of many nations" (recorded in Gen. 17:5, and referred to in Rom. 4:17)—is helpful here: "It is impossible to represent in the English the full force of the Greek, when the same word means *nations* and *Gentiles*."[5]

Saints: Those in Rome (and elsewhere) who had participated in obedience to the faith (or obedience of faith—16:26); those who had received grace (1:5). Adam Clarke L.L.D. contributes this rather complete summation of what the Gospel had accomplished in the lives of these Roman Christians, who had been called to be saints: "Invited to become holy persons, by believing the Gospel and receiving the gifts of the Holy Ghost. Or, here, the word may have the meaning of *made* or *constituted*, as above; constituted saints, for they had already received the Gospel grace, and were formed into a Christian Church."[6]

Boundless Spiritual Comfort Through Faith (1:8–12)

8 First, I thank my God through Jesus Christ for you all, that your faith is spoken of throughout the whole world.

9 For God is my witness, whom I serve with my spirit in the gospel of his Son, that without ceasing I make mention of you always in my prayers;

10 making request, if by any means now at length I might have a prosperous journey by the will of God to come unto you.

11 For I long to see you, that I may impart unto you some spiritual gift, to the end that you may be established;

12 That is, that I may be comforted together with you by the mutual faith both of you and me.

I recall the loneliness I once felt during my Brazilian missionary "tour" when I arrived at a bus stop in one of the northeast Brazil capitals and had to wait several hours for the next bus. Contemplating the distance between my family and me (they were in another country), I was deeply saddened—until I recalled the telephone conversation I had

had with my wife a couple of weeks earlier. Remembering the cheerfulness and optimism she had imparted gave me a new spirit. Instantly, the assurance of her presence comforted me!

The comfort of spirit that comes through faith is always available. This comfort is unbounded. Even before he could get there, Paul was already meaningfully engaged in his spirit with the Roman Christians: "Without ceasing I make mention of you always in my prayers" (v. 9). By what he knew was taking place in these Roman Christians, Paul could "thank God…for (them) all" (v. 8), even though he was not there. The most unmistakable life benefit of the through-Jesus-received-grace is this comforting, life-sustaining faith, this knowledge of God's calling and presence.

What did Paul mean when he said, "For I long to see you, that I may impart unto you some spiritual gift" (v. 11)? Joseph S. Exell contributes this helpful contextual consideration:

> The word he employs here, *gift*, is never used in the New Testament for a thing that one man can give to another, but is always employed for the concrete results of the grace of God bestowed upon men.[7]

Exell adds:

> Notice, too, as bearing on the limits of Paul's part in the gift, the delicacy of the language in his statement of the ultimate purpose of the gift. He does not say, "That I may strengthen you," which may have been too egotistical, but he says, "that ye may be strengthened" (in the King James Version, "established"), for the true strengthener is not Paul, but the Spirit of God.[8]

With reference to "that I may be comforted together with you" (v. 12), Exell writes:

> There were a few people inside Rome who believed in Jesus, and the apostle took courage from the thought that he should not be alone, but be surrounded by a loyal few. In the army everyone helps the other's courage. There is no talk about danger, but only of taking the battlements! So wherever you are, by the exercise of your faith you are sustaining that poor fellow there who has the same battle to fight as you have.[9]

A Compelling Motivation That Never Desists (1:13–17)

13 Now I would not have you ignorant, brethren, that oftentimes I purposed to come unto you, (but was let hitherto) that I might have some fruit among you also, even as among other Gentiles.

14 I am debtor both to the Greeks, and to the Barbarians; both to the wise, and to the unwise.

15 So, as much as in me is, I am ready to preach the gospel to you that are at Rome also.

16 For I am not ashamed of the gospel of Christ: for it is the power of God unto salvation to every one that believeth; to the Jew first, and also to the Greek.

17 For therein is the righteousness of God revealed from faith to faith: as it is written, The just shall live by faith.

A word is in order here about Paul's travel plans and how they figure into his fashioning of the epistle to the Romans. In the *Zondervan Pictorial Bible Dictionary*, James Oliver Buswell, Jr. sums it up this way:

The content and outline of this epistle must be understood from the point of view of Paul's total ministry and
his particular travel plans. True, the greatest theme in
the work is justification by faith. But this is not an essay
on that subject. Much of the material simply does not
fall under any sub-heading of that theme. This is a letter
from the apostle to the gentiles to the church in Rome,
and the subject is Why I Am Coming to Visit You.[10]

What is it that drove Paul, even to the extent of deter-
mining his travel destinations and how he would spend his
time? God's righteousness! The very possibility of it was
sufficient to dominate his thinking. And in Paul's thinking,
the pursuit of righteousness took in others by necessity:
"some fruit among you also" (v. 13). It was a debt that he
reckoned, and the preaching of the Gospel was the only
thing that would satisfy that debt, because it is the only thing
that reveals how God makes men righteous (1:16–17). But
how does the Gospel do that? By faith: "For therein is the
righteousness of God revealed from faith to faith; as it is
written, the just shall live by faith" (1:17). Regarding this
central theme of Romans, Buswell contributes this helpful
comment:

> It has been said that if Galatians is the "Magna Carta" of
> the Gospel, Romans is the "Constitution." The theologi-
> cal substance of this epistle had to be presented to the
> NT church, whether addressed to Rome or not, but there
> were circumstances in Rome which made it appropriate
> for Paul, in a relatively calm frame of mind, with time for
> fuller elaboration, and without having become personally
> involved in local affairs, as he had in Galatia, to expand
> the central doctrine of the epistle to the Galatians.[11]

In Romans, the apostle is not "too" anything: not too rushed, not too detached, and not too green. He has absolutely peaked! So while he zealously desired to be in the presence of his fellow saints, Paul meanwhile penned his meticulously complete Gospel: his epistle to the Romans.

In the same way that a drama narrator would break the ice by acquainting the spectators with himself, Paul likewise establishes common ground with the Roman saints (1:1–17). And in the same way that the narrator would conclude his preamble by decisively breaking forth with the drama's title (i.e., "And now…"), Paul likewise concludes his greetings with his decidedly arresting thematic statement: "The just shall live by faith." To the buttress of this platform, all the drama props are joisted. To the immortalizing of this irreplaceable truth, Paul directs his entire epistle.

James Macknight D.D. strongly vouches for the translation of verse 17 which emphasizes the part that trust—or faith—plays in the believer's accessibility to life:

> The just by faith shall live—They who are just by faith, shall live. This translation is agreeable both to the order of the words in the original, and to the apostle's design; which is to show that the doctrine of the gospel concerning righteousness, is attested even by the prophets.[12]

Clarke seconds this understanding of verse 17:

> This has been understood two ways: 1. That the just or righteous man cannot live a holy and useful life without exercising continual faith in our Lord Jesus: which is strictly true, for He only who has brought him into that state of salvation can preserve him in it; and he stands by faith. 2. It is contended by some able critics that the words of the original text should be pointed thus: The just by faith, shall live; that is, he alone that is justified by

9

faith shall be saved; which is also true; as it is impossible to get salvation in any other way. This last meaning is probably the true one, as the original text in Habakkuk 2:4 speaks of those who believed the declarations of God when the Chaldeans besieged Jerusalem, and, having acted conformably to them, escaped with their lives.[13]

Think about it. "The just"—the appeal is undeniable. "Shall live"—would you like that? "By faith"—it is within our reach. "The righteousness of God"—it conjures up a lot, but it is all right here. And the whole drama is going to be played out—in the next six chapters of Romans!

For Christ is the end of the law for righteousness to every one that believeth.

—Romans 10:4

CHAPTER 2

From Where We Came: The World of Sin (1:18–3:20)

THE CURTAIN TO our drama rises, and what can be seen is all sorts of disorder. God does not appear in any of the activity on the stage. Everyone is pursuing his own intention and running over the next person. The irreverence is unbelievable! It's as if no one has ever heard of God. It is open rebellion! Where could God be?

As we take in this stage activity, the floor gives way to a second group of a different type—in their dress and their countenance—and we sense this group's effort not to mix with the others. But we identify arrogance here as well. It's as though they were counting steps to make sure they've gotten everything just right.

Presently, we see the first group (the larger of the two) approach the different one. Because we now can encompass all of the activity on the stage, we begin to lose awareness of the second group—and the two become one.

What we witness in these first three chapters of Romans is the beginning of everything. The apostle's graphic images and the occasional "leap" (by way of Old Testament citations) from our time to theirs (from New Testament to Old Testament) parades the generations before us. It's hard to imagine a movie that would summon the emotions to equal the effect of Paul's words. The story of the Roman Christians begins here. The Gentiles take the stage in the beginning, but the Jews also will be players in Paul's drama.

Passage of time is the effect of Paul's exposition in these chapters: years of rebellion and years of striving in the law—and generation after generation of failure! And when we get to the end of this first scene, we still are where we started—in the world of sin.

But the apostle does not leave us there (and neither does God). Paul will continue forward until the present time. He will show what God has done. And Jesus Christ will become a part of our story. But we first have to learn from where we came.

The Withdrawal of Man and the Withdrawal of God (1:18–32)

> 18 For the wrath of God is revealed from heaven against all ungodliness and unrighteousness of men, who hold the truth in unrighteousness;
>
> 19 Because that which may be known of God is manifest in them; for God hath shewed it unto them.
>
> 20 For the invisible things of him from the creation of the world are clearly seen, being understood by the things that are made, even his eternal power and Godhead; so that they are without excuse:
>
> 21 Because that, when they knew God, they glorified him not as God, neither were thankful; but became vain in their imaginations, and their foolish heart was darkened.

22 Professing themselves to be wise, they became fools,

23 And changed the glory of the incorruptible God into an image made like to corruptible man, and to birds, and four-footed beasts, and creeping things.

The apostle's "for" ("For the wrath of God is revealed…") accelerates and turns Paul's epistle to the Romans to the preaching of the Gospel (v. 15), i.e., "the revelation of God's plan for reconciling man to Himself by forgiving his sin and by transforming his character" (see Glossary). This pivot is not slighted in Clarke's read on this verse:

> The apostle has now finished his preface, and comes to the grand subject of the epistle; namely, to show the absolute need of the Gospel of Christ, because of the universal corruption of mankind; which was so great as to incense the justice of God and call aloud for the punishment of the world. He shows that all the heathen nations were utterly corrupt, and deserved this threatened punishment. And this is the subject of the first chapter, from verse 18 to the end. He shows that the Jews, notwithstanding the greatness of their privileges, were no better than the Gentiles; and therefore the wrath of God was revealed against them also. This subject he treats in chap. 2 and chap. 3:1–19. He returns, as it were, on both, chap. 3:20–31, and proves that, as the Jews and Gentiles were equally corrupt, they could not be saved by the deeds of any law; that they stood equally in need of that salvation which God had provided; that both were equally entitled to that salvation, for God was the God of the Gentiles as well as of the Jews.[14]

God's revelation of His righteousness for man begins with a revelation of His wrath: "the wrath of God is revealed"

15

(v. 18). From the very beginning, quite a lot about God has been revealed to man: "God hath shewed it unto them" (v. 19). God's glory was revealed to man—the glory God intended for man. But man arrogantly pursued his own intentions: "changed the glory of the incorruptible God" (v. 23). Instead of allowing God's glory to run freely, man has "held" (covered up) the "truth" (about God's glory) by his own unrighteousness (v. 18). Man's character, by his own initiative, has been darkened (v. 21). And of the resulting communion between man's darkness and the divine glory? Read on.

24 Wherefore God also gave them up to uncleanness through the lusts of their own hearts, to dishonour their own bodies between themselves:

25 Who changed the truth of God into a lie, and worshipped and served the creature more than the Creator, who is blessed forever. Amen.

26 For this cause God gave them up unto vile affections: for even their women did change the natural use into that which is against nature:

27 And likewise also the men, leaving the natural use of the woman, burned in their lust one toward another; men with men working that which is unseemly, and receiving in themselves that recompence of their error which was meet.

God filled the world with His glory. And He made this evident to man: "That which may be known of God is manifest in them; for God hath shewed it unto them.... The invisible things of him...are clearly seen...when they knew God, they glorified him not as God" (1:19–21). It's not that man didn't know, it's that man openly went against his knowledge! He usurped the place of the Creator, putting himself above Him! The women and men changed the "natural use" (vv. 26 and 27). They left the natural use. And because of that, God left them: "For this cause God gave them up unto vile affections" (vv. 26 and 27).

> 28 And even as they did not like to retain God in their knowledge, God gave them over to a reprobate mind, to do those things which are not convenient;
>
> 29 Being filled with all unrighteousness, fornication, wickedness, covetousness, maliciousness; full of envy, murder, debate, deceit, malignity; whisperers,
>
> 30 Backbiters, haters of God, despiteful, proud, boasters, inventors of evil things, disobedient to parents,
>
> 31 without understanding, covenant breakers, without natural affection, implacable, unmerciful:
>
> 32 Who knowing the judgment of God, that they which commit such things are worthy of death, not only do the same, but have pleasure in them that do them.

God's self-manifestation is indispensable to us. Our history is evidence of the disregard of that manifestation—and the consequence of it: "God gave them over to a reprobate mind" (v. 28). Man withdrew, and then God withdrew. By his own initiative, man incurred enslavement to his passions—and to a life without God!

Two things are revealed—or manifested—early in Romans: God's righteousness (divinity; glory) and man's unrighteousness ("heart was darkened"—1:21). A great many of the Romans had come from this class of unrighteous men (1:5–6; 15:15–16). If you don't identify with this class, then hold on a minute. We have yet another class in God's story of our civilization.

17

The Desire to Do Good (2:1–11)

1 Therefore thou art inexcusable, o man, whosoever thou art that judgest: for wherein thou judgest another, thou condemnest thyself; for thou that judgest doest the same things.

2 But we are sure that the judgment of God is according to truth against them which commit such things.

3 And thinkest thou this, O man, that judgest them which do such things, and doest the same, that thou shalt escape the judgment of God?

4 Or despisest thou the riches of his goodness and forbearance and longsuffering; not knowing that the goodness of God leadeth thee to repentance?

5 But after thy hardness and impenitent heart treasurest up unto thyself wrath against the day of wrath and revelation of the righteous judgment of God;

6 Who will render to every man according to his deeds:

7 To them who by patient continuance in well doing seek for glory and honor and immortality, eternal life:

8 But unto them that are contentious, and do not obey the truth, but obey unrighteousness, indignation, and wrath,

9 Tribulation and anguish, upon every soul of man that doeth evil, of the Jew first, and also of the Gentile:

10 But glory, honour, and peace, to every man that worketh good, to the Jew first, and also to the Gentile:

11 For there is no respect of persons with God.

The thing this class has in common with the first is God's wrath: "But after thy hardness and impenitent heart treasurest up unto thyself wrath against the day of wrath"

18

(v. 5). And class doesn't matter, "for there is no respect of persons with God" (v. 11). But the deeds matter! And Paul's "good man" wants to do good. The fact that he "judges" proves this (v. 1). The irreverent type at the opening didn't even care; he already had thrown himself into the party!

The goal is so desirable: "glory and honour and immortality" (v. 7). And the intention is so good: "patient continuance in well doing" (v. 7). But it is so far from here to there: "Who will render to every man according to his deeds" (v. 6). What are we going to do with all this wrath? The whole thing is tiring, isn't it? The more I try, the more I condemn myself! But there is much more in this story.

Glossary

Truth: As used in verses two and eight, it has the meaning "what God has revealed."

Day of wrath: The day of God's judgment (v.5). God's wrath, however, resides in the lives of men who hold the truth in unrighteousness (1:18). See also John 8:36, where "the wrath of God abideth" is employed.

Immortality; eternal life: God's eternal quality that, at this point in Romans, is out of man's reach (v. 7).

The Law: That Scoundrel (2:12–29)

12 For as many as have sinned without law shall also perish without law: and as many as have sinned in the law shall be judged by the law;

13 (For not the hearers of the law are just before God, but the doers of the law shall be justified.

14 For when the Gentiles, which have not law, do by nature the things contained in the law, these, having not the law, are a law unto themselves:

19

15 Which shew the work of the law written in their hearts, their conscience also bearing witness, and their thoughts the meanwhile accusing or else excusing one another;)

16 In the day when God shall judge the secrets of men by Jesus Christ according to my gospel.

Here we see that the standard of goodness by which Paul's "good man" measures himself is the law. But not even to himself does he measure up: "as many as have sinned in the law shall be judged by the law" (v. 12). Within himself he doesn't feel justified; that is, that his deeds reach to the standard. (Paul projects this inner frustration in the parenthetical "For not the hearers of the law are just before God, but the doers of the law shall be justified"—v. 13). And the Gentiles—who don't have the law—are in this same living condemnation: "Their thoughts the meanwhile accusing or else excusing one another" (v. 15). There is nowhere to run! Always, the law is there. And it seems that all it wants to do is condemn. But…patience. Paul is only at the beginning of his story, and everything is following a track: "according to my gospel" (v. 16).

17 Behold, thou art called a Jew, and restest in the law, and makest thy boast of God,

18 And knowest his will, and approvest the things that are more excellent, being instructed out of the law;

19 And art confident that thou thyself art a guide of the blind, a light of them which are in darkness,

20 An instructor of the foolish, a teacher of babes, which hast the form of knowledge and of the truth in the law.

21 Thou therefore which teachest another, teachest thou not thyself? Thou that preachest a man should not steal, dost thou steal?

22 Thou that sayest a man should not commit adultery, dost thou commit adultery? Thou that abhorrest idols, dost thou commit sacrilege?

23 Thou that makest thy boast of the law, through breaking the law dishonorest thou God?

24 For the name of God is blasphemed among the Gentiles through you, as it is written.

There is no escaping God's wrath through revelation alone—either for the first class (the Gentiles) or the second class (the Jews). What the Jew had in the law was simply a more sophisticated level of revelation. And the law didn't show itself to be an ally of the Jew. Fact is, the law itself is what Paul employed to dismantle our second class: "Thou therefore which teachest another, teachest thou not thyself?" (v. 21). Do you recall Paul's accusation that pointed out the plight of the "good man"? "For thou that judgest doest the same things" (2:1). By his identification with the law, Paul's "good man" was self-condemning—because he couldn't keep the law!

But the law is not the culprit. The apparent stage blending (in the opening scene of our drama) between the two classes of people is due to the internal likeness of our players. Aside from their dress and ritual, the second class is identical to the first: They depend on themselves ("Thou that makest thy boast of the law"—v. 23). It's not the law that is the culprit. It is man's self-sufficiency—and self-dependence!

25 For circumcision verily profiteth, if thou keep the law: but if thou be a breaker of the law, thy circumcision is made uncircumcision.

26 Therefore if the uncircumcision keep the righteousness of the law, shall not his uncircumcision be counted for circumcision?

27 And shall not uncircumcision which is by nature, if it fulfill the law, judge thee, who by the letter and circumcision dost transgress the law?

28 For he is not a Jew, which is one outwardly; neither is that circumcision, which is outward in the flesh:

29 But he is a Jew, which is one inwardly; and circumcision is that of the heart, in the spirit, and not in the letter; whose praise is not of men, but of God.

Our stage has turned homogeneous! The first class—the irreverent ones (here designated as "uncircumcision")—is even judging the good: "Shall not uncircumcision which is by nature if it fulfill the law judge thee, who by the letter and circumcision dost transgress the law?" (v. 27).

"But I want to do right," the good man says to himself. "I want to be good, and I'm not able to!" There is so much emphasis on the deeds…could it be that God gave us something that is too hard?

But wait a minute! Is there a way for one to be recompensed for his goodwill, his desire to do good? He would be trusting, in that way, in another who could appropriate. Is there a way to overcome this inability of the flesh? Could it be that God could come to see what is in one's heart? Does every man (and woman) have an equal right to want to be a "Jew inwardly" (vv. 28 and 29)? Is it realistic for people to picture themselves being made righteous if they want that and trust they will receive it? Continue reading.

Glossary

Law: Can mean "Law of Moses," or simply *law* (i.e., any "law"). Romans 2:14 illustrates these two uses of "law," distinguished by the definite pronoun. Paul's point is that all law condemns, hence the chief teaching in Romans is "the just shall live by faith" (Rom. 1:16–17). This powerful assertion from God is given no less than four times in God's self-revelation to man: Habakkuk 2:4; Romans 1:17; Galatians 3:11; and Hebrews 10:38.

Jew: The Jew was, by design (in relation to the Law of Moses), actually a "guide...a light...an instructor ..." (2:19–20). Paul himself affirms this distinction: "The gospel...is the power of God unto salvation to every one that believeth; to the Jew first..." (1:16). What Paul is demonstrating in Romans 1–3 is that all (Gentiles and Jews) are unrighteous—with law (Jews) and without law (Gentiles).

Circumcision: More than the physical act, the term indicates a relationship of a people (Jews) with the Law of Moses. *Judaism* is a comparable term.

Uncircumcision: The state of being outside the Jewish circle. *Circumcision* and *uncircumcision* were abolished in Christ (Gal. 5:2–6; 3:26–28; 6:14–16; Eph. 2:11–22).

Letter: The religious attention to the precepts of the law. "Human effort without the grace of God."

Flesh: Has to do with the human side, in contradistinction to the spiritual side (that is, what proceeds from God).

God's Just Judgment (3:1–8)

1 What advantage then hath the Jew? Or what profit is there of circumcision?

2 Much every way: chiefly, because that unto them were committed the oracles of God.

3 For what if some did not believe? Shall their unbelief make the faith of God without effect?

23

4 God forbid: yea, let God be true, but every man a liar; as it is written, That thou mightest be justified in thy sayings, and mightest overcome when thou art judged.

5 But if our unrighteousness commend the righteousness of God, what shall we say? Is God unrighteous who taketh vengeance? (I speak as a man.)

6 God forbid; for then how shall God judge the world?

7 For if the truth of God hath more abounded through my lie unto his glory; why yet am I also judged as a sinner?

8 And not rather, (as we be slanderously reported, and as some affirm that we say,) Let us do evil, that good may come? Whose damnation is just.

The curtain in our drama drops, giving us a breather. When it rises again, we have a single player: a narrator (in Romans, the apostle Paul). He speaks, initially, for the Jew (3:1), then for God (3:2–4), then a second time for the Jew (3:5), and likewise, a second time for God (3:6–8). Paul, in this simulated dialogue, defends God's condemnation of the Jew. (Remember that it is God Himself who is really telling this story [1:1].) Then, to drive the message home, our narrator paces off the distance to the rear stage exit, and summarizes in brusque, unforgettable words (Rom. 3:9–20) the case against "both Jews and Gentiles" (3:9), declaring that "all the world [is]...guilty before God" (3:19). "They are all under sin" (3:9).

But why does the apostle feel constrained to defend God's righteousness and His just judgment? Do you recall from the beginning in "the world of sin" the statement, "The wrath of God is revealed...against all...unrighteousness of men" (1:18), and again (referring to the "good man"), "Therefore thou art inexcusable, o man, whosoever thou

24

art that judgest...but after thy hardness and impenitent heart treasurest up unto thyself wrath against the day of wrath" (2:1, 5)? If God is going to condemn even people like these Jews, who were as seriously religious as what we have seen, then God Himself is going to have to be perfectly righteous. And He opens Himself up to this kind of examination. But watch out! God is going to prevail. His wrath will prove to be justified. And the Jew, with his irresponsible "blame-gaming," confirms this. It will not do for the Jew to say, "He picked on us"! Instead, each one of them ought to have sought His will.

Glossary

The Oracles of God (3:2): The Law of Moses that was given to the Israelite nation (Jews) at the base of Mt. Sinai. (Exodus 19:1–5; 20:1–17; **Acts 7:38**)

All the World Guilty Before God (3:9–20)

9 What then? Are we better than they? No, in no wise: for we have before proved both Jews and Gentiles, that they are all under sin;

10 As it is written, There is none righteous, No, not one;

11 There is none that understandeth, there is none that seeketh after God.

12 They are all gone out of the way, they are together become unprofitable; there is none that doeth good, no, not one.

13 Their throat is an open sepulchre; with their tongues they have used deceit; the poison of asps is under their lips:

14 Whose mouth is full of cursing and bitterness:

25

15 Their feet are swift to shed blood:

16 Destruction and misery are in their ways:

17 And the way of peace they have not known:

18 There is no fear of God before their eyes.

19 Now we know that what things soever the law saith, it saith to them that are under the law: that every mouth may be stopped, and all the world may become guilty before God.

20 Therefore by the deeds of the law there shall no flesh be justified in his sight: for by the law is the knowledge of sin.

There is a marked somberness to the close of our first act (Rom. 1:18–3:20). The auditorium lights have been dimmed, and all of the players and their activity have disappeared. All that remains is a single narrator, and his countenance communicates gravity. As he turns and walks toward the rear exit of the stage, he begins to speak. (In our drama, this scene is framed by 3:9–20). In a deep voice that strikes the very core of our being, he utters some lines that remind us of a dirge. And with each step, the darkness deepens—and so does the dirge. We expect that at any moment the lights will return, the activity will return, and everything will be normal. Only, that doesn't happen. Instead, the narrator exits the door at the rear of the stage, leaves us in the darkness—and the curtain drops!

The world of sin—it is a reality that reaches us all. And our sinning has not been light! The description in these verses is without comparison in its graphic image. The effect of the Old Testament citations—delivered in rapid succession—is to remove the barrier of time and group the whole world under the condemnation: We are sinners!

There is none righteous. We are "all gone out of the way" (3:12).

In this narrated section (3:1–20), Paul first addresses his compatriots, the Jews: "What advantage then hath the Jew?" (3:1). Paul also closes with the Jews: "What things the law saith it saith to them that are under the law" (v. 19). Paul does this so "that every mouth may be stopped, and all the world may become guilty before God" (v. 19).

God's self-revelation to the Gentiles didn't turn them in His direction (1:18–32). Despite a more sophisticated revelation through the law, communion also was not realized between the Jews and God (chapter 2). And as unequivocally concluded in 3:9–20, law of no sort will bring about this communion: "By the deeds of the law shall no flesh be justified in his sight; for by the law is the knowledge of sin" (v. 20). All of mankind is in an extreme need for a Savior.

CHAPTER 3

The Manifestation of Righteousness in This Present Time (3:21–4:25)

OUR DRAMA BEGINS Act Two destitute of players. When the curtain rises, all that can be seen is a large projection screen, centrally located on the stage. Without any outside prompting, the screen begins to communicate with us in the audience. Simultaneously, voices and people appear on the screen. The sound from the screen increases, attracting our attention. Shortly, we begin to recognize the happenings on the screen: They are the activities of the Gentiles, the irreverent type from the beginning of the drama. We notice at the same time that some of the players (the Gentile actors) enter the stage and line up along the sideline, watching the screen.

The activity on the screen moves on to the Jewish drama—with all their attention to ritual and details. And we notice a second group—the Jewish actors—enters the stage and lines up along the other side, looking (as the first group did) at the screen.

Romans 3:21 abruptly interrupts Paul's dissertation on sin, which began in 1:18. Beginning here, the apostle gives us a manifestation of God's righteousness. It's as if a revelation is being made to us—something akin to "Breaking News" appearing on TV. The law didn't provide the righteousness man sought (chapters 2 and 3). God will now remove this law and send Jesus Christ to step into our history and become man's object of faith. In Christ, God gives man the perfect fulfillment of the law (Rom. 10:4). Beginning here, the idea that the just shall live by faith (1:17) is dissected in the book of Romans. By faith in God's Son, man will be able to receive God's righteousness.

After Jesus Christ, Paul uses another historical personage— Abram (Abraham)—to give evidence that by faith (trust), God's righteousness is given to man (4:1–25). In chapters 3 and 4, grace begins to distinguish itself. Additionally, Paul begins to employ hope in his story of man's justification. So far, our drama hasn't generated much reason for hope—but that was before this manifestation of God's free favor of righteousness!

God's Provision (3:21–31)

21 But now the righteousness of God without the law is manifested, being witnessed by the law and the prophets;

22 Even the righteousness of God which is by faith of Jesus Christ unto all and upon all them that believe: for there is no difference:

23 For all have sinned, and come short of the glory of God;

24 Being justified freely by his grace through the redemption that is in Christ Jesus:

25 Whom God hath set forth to be a propitiation through faith in his blood, to declare, I say, at this time his

righteousness: that he might be just, and the justifier of
him which believeth in Jesus.

27 Where is boasting then? It is excluded. By what law?
Of works? Nay: but by the law of faith.

28 Therefore we conclude that a man is justified by faith
without the deeds of the law.

29 Is he the God of the Jews only? Is he not also of the
Gentiles? Yes, of the Gentiles also:

30 Seeing it is one God, which shall justify the circumcision by faith, and uncircumcision through faith.

31 Do we then make void the law through faith? God
forbid: Yea, we establish the law.

"But now…" (v. 21). The announcement from the projection screen abruptly closes the most complete discussion on
sin to be found in the New Testament. The announcement
also brings to an end the discussion of things past. "This
now is in the present!" is the force of the declaration. The
mere mention of a change gives us hope!

"The righteousness of God without the law is manifested" (v. 21): The good news from the projection screen
continues. (The law sure wasn't any road we wanted to
travel.) After all the effort in the law (and all the failures!),
now—without any help from man— God's righteousness
is manifested, as if appearing on a screen. And we in the
audience can just see our players straining to catch every
word proceeding from the screen.

The headlines on the screen continue: "Being witnessed
by the law and the prophets" (v. 21). At this point, we begin
to witness on the screen a review—in rapid succession—of
all the activities we have seen in the drama: The two groups
(or "classes"), the separation of the second group from
the first, and the deaths of several animals of sacrifice.

31

Suddenly everything on the screen stops—the noise of the sacrificed animals, everything! And when we think that the stage spectators (our players) verily have halted their breathing, a cross appears on the screen—a huge, red cross that completely fills the screen. Then the announcement continues, proceeding from the screen.

"Even the righteousness of God which is by faith of Jesus Christ unto all…that believe…being justified freely by his grace" (vv. 22, 24): man sought it and didn't find it. And now, completely gratuitously, it has been offered to man. With this announcement, man becomes a recipient of God's free favor of righteousness (i.e., His grace)! And the work in this justification (or salvation) of man—who does this? And man—what is his part in this justification?

But we have much more drama remaining! The headlines on the screen continue. "Through the redemption that is in Christ Jesus, whom God hath set forth to be a propitiation through faith in his blood" (vv. 24, 25).

"Ohh… I see!" we say to ourselves. "God's righteousness (for man) involves Christ Jesus, redemption, and the blood of Jesus." We in the audience almost can see the understanding revealed in the expressions of the stage spectators (the players observing the screen).

Once again, the announcement on the screen picks back up. "That he might be just, and the justifier of him which believeth in Jesus" (v. 25). At this point, several of our stage spectators shake hands and pat the backs of others in their group, and then turn and do the same with members of the other group. The justification, they come to understand, is for all who trust and avail themselves of this redemption on the cross through Christ's blood! "Thank God for His grace!" is what the players' smiles seem to be saying.

As the screen goes blank, the narrator returns, positions himself between the two projection screen spectator groups, joins hands with one player on the right and one on the left, and, along with all the players, proclaims: "Therefore we conclude that a man is justified by faith without the deeds of the law" (v. 28). And the curtain falls.

Glossary

Prophets: Refers to the writings of the prophets (in the Old Testament).

Justified: Counted as righteous; one to whom God does not impute sin.

Redemption: To buy back again (see Eph. 1:6–7).

Propitiation: Satisfaction for sins (i.e., payment for sins) or that which satisfies (see 1 John 2:1–2).

The Evidence in Abram (4:1–25)

From behind the curtain, our narrator reads the opening lines of the Abraham scene:

1 What shall we say then that Abraham our father, as pertaining to the flesh, hath found?

2 For if Abraham were justified by works, he hath whereof to glory; but not before God.

3 For what saith the scripture? Abraham believed God, and it was counted unto him for righteousness.

4 Now to him that worketh is the reward not reckoned of grace, but of debt.

5 But to him that worketh not, but believeth on him that justifieth the ungodly, his faith is counted for righteousness.

6 Even as David also describeth the blessedness of the man, unto whom God imputeth righteousness without works,

7 Saying, Blessed are they whose iniquities are forgiven, and whose sins are covered.

8 Blessed is the man to whom the Lord will not impute sin.

"What shall we say then that Abraham our father, as pertaining to the flesh, hath found" (v. 1)? This is one of those abrupt interruptions that gives Romans its dramatic presence. The "but now" interruption of 3:21 likewise has been referenced. Right in the middle of a doctrinal soliloquy, the apostle jumps out of his personal space and into our personal lives! It's not that this is foreign to the Bible narrative elsewhere. Malachi employed this with the readers of his prophecy in Malachi 1:6–7; 2:13–14, 17; 3:8.

Jesus used this projected questioning very dramatically and effectively in Matthew 25:34–40, et. al.

But this dramatic presentation of the Gospel takes center stage in Romans! It is unsurpassed in realism, pertinence, and impact. An even halfway serious reading of it gives a whole new appreciation for what was behind Paul's introductory remark, "So, as much as in me is, I am ready to preach the gospel to you that are at Rome also" (1:15).

"Abram!" "Abram!" From the four corners of the ceiling comes the voice. The curtain begins to rise. What we see on the stage is a single man, advanced in years and of rustic attire. Draped over his shoulder is a type of shawl, having the appearance of animal skins. He has a head wrap that hangs free to just below the back of his neck. Beneath the cover of a beard, his look is one of determination. The cane he dons does not convey weakness, for his posture is erect and his head squarely set on his shoulders. As he walks, his hardened sandals click with each step, giving the impression of weight and strain. Even so, we sense he could—if he wanted—travel this way the entire day.

"Abram!" "Abram!" At the sound of the voice, the man stops, inclines his head in the direction of the voice, and, after a brief period of time in which we sense something was communicated to him, kneels and lifts his eyes and hands in the direction of the voice. Directly, he rests his arms. As he lowers his eyesight, he spots a stone. He picks it up, sets it before him, and then stands and walks, picking up a stone here and a stone there. He then begins to pile the stones as if to build a crude altar. While this is going on, a second man (our narrator) enters the stage, walking in our direction, and stops at the front of the stage, as the lights are dimmed over "Abram" and his altar. Then the narrator (in our story, the apostle Paul) starts:

"What shall we say then that Abraham our father, as pertaining to the flesh, hath found?" (v. 1). ("Father... pertaining to the flesh" is an obvious reference to the Romans who were Jews.) As in 3:1–8, Paul is speaking for the Jews. He can imagine that with all this new manifestation of justification by faith in Jesus, the Jews must be thinking, *What, then, of Abraham and his works...and the law? What, even, of the Old Testament?* To answer this, Paul goes directly to "what saith the scripture." And what does it say? Abraham believed God, and it was counted unto him for righteousness (v. 3). There's nothing here of intelligence on Paul's part; nothing of human wisdom. The proof of the announcement on the screen (the manifestation of righteousness by faith) hangs on "what saith the scripture." And Paul doesn't limit himself to this or that epoch. He goes all the way back to the first Jew: Abram. Righteousness by faith counted for Abram, too! Abram believed...and was justified. And that's that! Notice the weight Garland Elkins places on "what saith the scripture":

> Romans affirms not only that the prophets were prophets of God, but also that it is in the scriptures they wrote that we learn of the promise of the gospel. God "promised afore through his prophets in the Holy Scriptures" the gospel (Rom. 1:2). The same apostles and prophets who affirm, in the New Testament, that Christ died for our sins affirm that the Old Testament is inspired. Romans quotes the Old Testament and views it as God's word.[15]

"Abram!" "Abram!" The light once again illuminates the stage portion where Abram and the altar are. "Abram! I have made thee a father of many nations."

Abram raises his eyes in a thoughtful way, picks up the finishing stone, and lays it on his altar. And the light once again focuses on our narrator.

37

9 Cometh this blessedness then upon the circumcision only, or upon the uncircumcision also? For we say that faith was reckoned to Abraham for righteousness.

10 How was it then reckoned? When he was in circumcision, or in uncircumcision? Not in circumcision, but in uncircumcision.

11 And he received the sign of circumcision, a seal of the righteousness of the faith which he had yet being uncircumcised: that he might be the father of all them that believe, though they be not circumcised; that righteousness might be imputed unto them also:

12 And the father of circumcision to them who are not of the circumcision only, but who also walk in the steps of that faith of our father Abraham, which he had being yet uncircumcised.

13 For the promise, that he should be heir of the world, was not to Abraham, or to his seed, through the law, but through the righteousness of faith.

14 For if they which are of the law be heirs, faith is made void, and the promise made of none effect:

15 Because the law worketh wrath: for where no law is, there is no transgression.

16 Therefore it is of faith that it might be by grace; to the end the promise might be sure to all the seed; not to that only which is of the law, but to that also which is of the faith of Abraham; who is the father of us all.

17 (As it is written, I have made Thee a father of many nations,) before him whom he believed, even God, who quickeneth the dead, and calleth those things which be not as though they were.

God made a promise to Abraham: he would be "the father of all them that believe" (v. 11), because Abraham believed and was justified. Abraham was the first in the line. Thus he became the standard by reason of "what saith the scripture" and the promise God made to Abraham. Man's salvation originates from that trio: God-Abraham-promise (Gal. 3:6–8). Jesus Christ Himself is a product of this trio (Gal. 3:16).

But the Jews had an affinity to the law. Despite all their frustration in the law (chapters 2 and 3), Paul still sees a tendency in that direction. In this section, he makes an appeal for the Jews to consider "what saith the scripture"—of the justification of Abraham and of the promise.

What the scripture "saith" is Abraham's faith was counted unto him for righteousness (4:3). "How was it then reckoned?" (v. 10). As our narrator asks the question from the front of the stage, we can sense the conviction in his voice. "When he was in circumcision, or in uncircumcision? Not in circumcision, but in uncircumcision," he continues. "And he received the sign of circumcision, a seal of the righteousness of the faith which he had yet being uncircumcised: that he might be the father of all them that believe, though they be not circumcised; that righteousness might be imputed unto them also" (v. 11). Abraham was justified by faith without anything else! At that time, he didn't have circumcision, he didn't have the law—nothing! Just faith. And this sufficed. And this will suffice for all who believe in that which "saith the scripture." As Clarke says:

> For Abraham, the father and founder of the Jewish people, was justified by faith, before even the law was given; and by believing, in reference to the spiritual object held forth in the various ordinances of the law, and now revealed under the Gospel, he and all his believing descendants have been justified. And thus the faith of the old covenant led on to the faith of the new covenant,

which shows that salvation has been by faith from the call of Abraham to the present time.[16]

From Abraham, the narrator—the apostle Paul—turns to a consideration of the promise. "For the promise, that he should be heir of the world, was not to Abraham, or to his seed, through the law, but through the righteousness of faith" (v. 13). None of this originated in Paul. Everything is from that which "saith the scripture." But the apostle does pull out all the stops and appeal to a close friend: the knowledge within the Romans themselves. Paul is really preaching! "Think about this!" he is saying.

"For if they which are of the law be heirs, faith is made void, and the promise made of none effect" (v. 14). He is appealing to their logic, but it is the following declarative that really stabs their hearts. "Because the law worketh wrath: for where no law is, there is no transgression!" (v. 15). The Gospel works like that: It convicts the person of guilt, but then it scampers after the person to fill him or her with assurance and hope.

Our narrator proceeds: "Therefore it is of faith, that it might be by grace; to the end the promise might be sure to all the seed; not to that only which is of the law, but to that also which is of the faith of Abraham; who is the father of us all, as it is written, I have made thee a father of many nations." God made a promise. And that promise will stand—but not by the law. The promise didn't originate in the law. It doesn't operate by law, but through the righteousness of faith ("The just shall live by faith"—1:17). This is in accordance with grace, which denotes not only that the righteousness of faith (v. 13) proceeds from God, but that it is guaranteed by God "to the end the promise might be sure to all the seed" (v. 16). It really convinces, doesn't it? God's righteousness is available to all, provided we receive it through faith and from grace.

The curtain drops, giving us a breather to assimilate all the facts. Presently, from behind the curtain, the narrator begins reading the closing lines from the Abraham scene:

> 17 (As it is written, I have made thee a father of many nations,) before him whom he believed, even God, who quickeneth the dead, and calleth those things which be not as though they were.
>
> 18 Who against hope believed in hope, that he might become the father of many nations, according to that which was spoken, So shall thy seed be.
>
> 19 And being not weak in faith, he considered not his own body now dead, when he was about a hundred years old, neither yet the deadness of Sara's womb:
>
> 20 He staggered not at the promise of God through unbelief; but was strong in faith, giving glory to God;
>
> 21 and being fully persuaded that, what he had promised, he was able also to perform.
>
> 22 And therefore it was imputed to him for righteousness.
>
> 23 Now it was not written for his sake alone, that it was imputed to him;
>
> 24 But for us also, to whom it shall be imputed, if we believe on him that raised up Jesus our Lord from the dead;
>
> 25 Who was delivered for our offences, and was raised again for our justification.

"Abraham!" "Abraham!" When the curtain rises, the stage lights reveal an older Abraham. His hair has grayed, his clothing shows wear, and his posture reveals the setting

41

in of fatigue. (His cane is laboring a bit.) The altar is still in the scene, but it too shows signs of time. It is a moving scene! We feel as though we have known this man a long time.

"Abraham! I have made thee a father of many nations" (v. 17). Abraham raises his eyes, meditates several seconds, and then starts to turn, when the voice returns, interrupting his intention.

"Abraham! So shall thy seed be" (v. 18). Abraham inclines in the direction of the voice, and—with the aid of his cane—does a slow pirouette, while looking up at the sky. Then, as if to take care of something, our Abraham hurriedly leaves while we are left contemplating the altar and the empty stage.

While we still are caught up in our thoughts about Abraham, the stage lights once again reveal our narrator, who is at the front of the stage. He has one hand on the corner of a podium and the other is supporting his chin, giving him a thoughtful countenance. His body is turned so as to give him full view of the altar.

The narrator is the final player in the Abraham scene. Looking the whole time at the altar, he sums up the encounter between God and Abraham. At the close, he turns in our direction (the audience) and makes a direct application of this Abraham scene to himself and to us. The curtain then drops, giving us an intermission, after which the narrator returns and begins to tell us of a second historical figure: Jesus Christ.

In just one chapter (chapter 4), much has happened. We have come to know Abraham well. In this final scene, there is not one mention of law or circumcision. The whole thing started with only God, a man, and a promise. In this last scene, all that remains are these three. Beginning with this trio, the story of hope can be told to mankind. That's because God's free favor of righteousness offer came from this trio!

Why did Abraham believe? It occurred to me, in reading this chapter, that Paul didn't say much about that—until I discovered verse 17: "before him whom he believed." Think about it: Abraham came before Him—face to face with God! Either visibly, or entirely in the form of a voice, Abraham had an encounter with God...and he believed! As Elkins explains:

> When one looked at the physical conditions (the age of both Sarah and of Abraham) apart from the promise of God there was no natural ground on which to hope for a descendant through Sarah. However, because Abraham had faith in God and His word ("So shall thy seed be"), he had a hope based not on human reason but on the divine revelation....Abraham's faith was based on what God had promised. Too often there are people who have a strong conviction that God will do what they have promised themselves or what someone else has promised them. We must be sure that we are basing our faith on what God has said. And unless we can find it in His word, we cannot scripturally claim that God will perform it.[17]

The apostle Paul has been telling us that God is near and available for examination: "That which may be known of God is manifest in them...for the invisible things of him from the creation of the world are clearly seen, being understood by the things that are made" (Rom. 1:19–21). In Jesus Christ, God came very near for examination. In Christ, God made very real—for you and me—the possibility of an encounter with God!

Our narrator has now arrived at the close of his summation: "Being fully persuaded that what he had promised, he was able also to perform. And therefore it was imputed to him for righteousness" (vv. 21–22). The narrator pauses, looks directly at the audience, and adds: "Now it was not written for his sake alone, that it was imputed to him; But for us also, to whom it shall be imputed, if we believe on him that raised up Jesus our Lord from the dead, who was delivered for our offences, and was raised again for our justification" (vv. 23–25).

And the curtain falls.

For whatsoever things were written aforetime were written for our learning, that we through patience and comfort of the scriptures might have hope.

—Romans 15:4

CHAPTER 4

Righteousness and Life from Grace (5:1-21)

*A*FTER AN INTERMISSION, the curtain again rises. What we see facing us is a line of people that spans the width of the stage. By their clothing, we begin to recognize some of them: They are the players from past scenes. And they are all mixed—Jews and Gentiles together. Just then, another person comes on the stage—our narrator—and joins himself to the group, taking the place in the center. Without any perceivable cue, they start with a single voice, an exuberant, well-anticipated refrain:

> Therefore being justified by faith, we have peace with God through our Lord Jesus Christ, by whom also we have access by faith into this grace wherein we stand, and we rejoice in hope of the glory of God.
> —Romans 5:1,2

In the audience, we are not quite prepared for the jump from the Abraham scene to this one. Even with the intermission and the mention of Jesus Christ at the end of the Abraham scene, we are still there, captivated by Abraham.

47

Keep in mind that in the epistle to the Romans, Paul is announcing the Gospel to readers who had already been told the story of Christ. They were already the called of Jesus Christ (1:5–7). In his eagerness to be with them (15:22–24), Paul is telling—in the meantime—the whole story again. And we *will* have the whole story. Paul will dissect the work of Christ, shortly!

But it is impressive, really, the evidence Abraham provides. It is so much so that Paul can't conclude the encounter between God and Abraham without proclaiming: "Therefore being justified by faith, we have peace with God!" Clarke says:

> The Apostle takes it for granted that he has proved that justification is by faith, and that the Gentiles have an equal title with the Jews to salvation by faith. And now he proceeds to show the effects produced in the hearts of the believing Gentiles by this doctrine.[18]

Finally! After all the failed attempts—peace with God! The righteousness that to Abraham was imputed by faith, also will be imputed to us "if we believe on him who raised up Jesus our Lord from the dead, who was delivered for our offenses and raised again for our justification" (4:24–25). This last declaration (v. 25) is what comprises the theme of Romans 5: the work of Christ in our salvation. And this "work" makes up God's grace! The apostle conducts us from the faith demonstrated in Abraham (chapter 4) to the grace demonstrated in Christ (chapter 5).

In the lives of the Roman readers to whom Paul wrote this letter, we are now in the present—that is, at their actual reading of Paul's letter. The past would have been when they were in the world of sin (1:18–3:20)—either as a Gentile or striving in the law as a Jew. "And why," we might ask, "relive all that?" (as Paul does, here in Romans). In chapter 5, you will see why. What we know of the past helps us in the present. If Jesus did something for these Romans, then it is quite certain He will continue to do that, provided they continue to trust. The grace doesn't stop. These Romans needed to know that. But I'm getting ahead of myself. Keep reading.

Being Now Justified, We Shall Be Saved (5:1–11)

1 Therefore being justified by faith, we have peace with God through our Lord Jesus Christ:

2 By whom also we have access by faith into this grace wherein we stand, and rejoice in hope of the glory of God.

3 And not only so, but we glory in tribulations also: knowing that tribulation worketh patience;

4 And patience, experience; and experience, hope:

5 and hope maketh not ashamed; because the love of God is shed abroad in our hearts by the Holy Ghost which is given unto us.

What is the origin of hope? It is born of experience. Hope has to originate in the past. In other words, it has to be created. It doesn't originate from itself. And if the past is all bad, then there is no hope.

But God changes our past, because we can't do that. He justifies, which is to say, "You are guilty, but I'm not going to take that into account. Instead, I'm going to attribute righteousness to you." He changes our past, and this creates hope. God makes our experience good! And all of the succeeding difficulties (tribulations) prompt us to persevere, which further gives us a good experience and winds up creating more—you guessed it—hope. But all of

49

this has to have a beginning, an origin. In Jesus Christ, God creates this origin. "We have peace with God," Paul says, "through our Lord Jesus Christ" (5:1).

It's impressive, really, how much our experience influences our hope. "And hope maketh not ashamed," Paul says in verse 5. It doesn't let us down—that is, promise one thing and do another. Paul continues: "Because the love of God is shed abroad in our hearts" (v. 5). The verb tense ("is shed") suggests evidence that never goes away: "Everywhere we turn, we 'experience' the love of God!" is what Paul is saying. The Christian's "experience" will always be productive—creating hope!

> 6 For when we were yet without strength, in due time Christ died for the ungodly.
>
> 7 For scarcely for a righteous man will one die: yet peradventure for a good man some would even dare to die.
>
> 8 But God commendeth his love toward us, in that, while we were yet sinners, Christ died for us.
>
> 9 much more then, being now justified by his blood, we shall be saved from wrath through him.
>
> 10 For if, when we were enemies, we were reconciled to God by the death of his Son, much more, being reconciled, we shall be saved by his life.
>
> 11 And not only so, but we also joy in God through our Lord Jesus Christ, by whom we have now received the atonement.

Paul continues hammering away on this good experience (or evidence) of the past: "God commendeth his love toward us, in that, while we were yet sinners, Christ died for us....When we were enemies, we were reconciled to

God" (vv. 8–10). Our players and narrator now get to the end of their refrain:

> Much more, being reconciled, we shall be saved by his life. And not only so, but we also joy in God through our Lord Jesus Christ, by whom we have now received the atonement (vv. 10–11).

With this last line, the players part, leaving the narrator on the stage alone. He clears his throat, drops his arms in a gesture of relaxation, and—perceiving that the audience desires to hear more about this "Lord Jesus Christ"—motions for silence.

For the reader unaccustomed to Romans, its first four chapters may appear somewhat cold. The announcement of the Gospel has been logical, well ordered, and even convincing—but not very moving. That's because Christ was absent from our Gospel! Elkins explains:

> Although it is scriptural to speak of the plan of salvation, for God's purpose was not unfolded and carried out in a planless way, it must never be forgotten that the gospel is not a set of cold, impersonal principles, but centers in the person, Jesus Christ. It is "the gospel of God… concerning his Son"(1:1–2). Without the Son of God there is no gospel of salvation and there is no hope of anyone becoming a child of God through the new birth. What does Christianity have that other religions do not have? It can be briefly summed up in the answer, Christ.[19]

In the introduction to his story, Paul said, "The gospel of Christ…is the power of God unto salvation…for therein is the righteousness of God revealed" (1:16,17). If you leave out Jesus Christ from this revelation of righteousness, you don't have anything that saves. The appeal—the power—of the Gospel resides in the story of Jesus! And it was this that changed the story of the Romans and can change your story. The apostle has included in Romans (you guessed right!) the whole story. Please, keep reading!

In chapter 5, God's love takes center stage in Paul's drama. Is there any difference between God's love and God's grace? In chapter 4, we saw that righteousness was attributed to Abraham—that is, by the goodness or grace of God. Could we say God loved Abraham? Here in 5:2, Paul refers to "this grace wherein we stand." From there he goes on to talk about the "love of God…shed abroad in our hearts" (v. 5). Was it love or grace that sent Christ to the cross? There isn't much difference. "Love" is even rendered occasionally as "charity" (which comes from the Greek *karis*, for "grace"). In common speech, we have the expression "by the love of God" and also "by the grace of God." There isn't much difference in the two. Alexander Maclaren D.D. says:

> After all is said and done, the love of God, eternal, self-originated, the source of all Christian experiences because of the work of Christ which originates them all, is the root fact of the universe, and the guarantee that our highest anticipations and desires are not unsubstantial visions, but morning dreams, which are proverbially sure to be fulfilled. God is love; therefore the man who trusts Him shall not be put to shame.[20]

The point Paul is making is that God's goodness (or love or grace) is such that "while we were yet sinners, Christ died for us" (v. 8). If He loved us that much, if His grace sufficed for the Romans in the past, will it not equally do so from here on?

Glossary

Holy Spirit: Its first mention in Romans is here in verse five. The Holy Spirit was given to Paul and the Roman saints. The Scriptures elsewhere testify that the Holy Spirit is given to those who obey God (Acts 5:32). "Obedience" is the subject of chapter 6.

Atonement: Translated also as "reconciliation" (NASV and others). The term indicates the restoration of peace.

Shall Reign in Life by One (5:12–21)

12 Wherefore, as by one man sin entered into the world, and death by sin; and so death passed upon all men, for that all have sinned:

13 (For until the law sin was in the world: but sin is not imputed when there is no law.

14 Nevertheless death reigned from Adam to Moses, even over them that had not sinned after the similitude of Adam's transgression, who is the figure of him that was to come.

15 But not as the offence, so also is the free gift. For if through the offence of one many be dead, much more the grace of God, and the gift by grace, which is by one man, Jesus Christ, hath abounded unto many.

16 And not as it was by one that sinned, so is the gift: for the judgment was by one to condemnation but the free gift is of many offences unto justification.

17 For if by one man's offence death reigned by one; much more they which receive abundance of grace and of the gift of righteousness shall reign in life by one, Jesus Christ.)

Following my delivery of a sermon on Acts 2, in which I accentuated our responsibility in Christ's death (which responsibility Peter, in Acts 2, also laid on the Jews), a young man approached me and commented, "I don't think there are very many people who feel like their sins are 'responsible' for the death of Christ. Mostly, they consider Christ's death as simply an act of human suffering." But at the close of the Abraham scene (4:23–25), Paul said, "It was not written for his (Abraham's) sake alone, that it was imputed to him, but for us also, to whom it shall be imputed, if we believe on him that raised up Jesus our Lord from the dead, who was delivered for our offences."

Jesus Christ was crucified for our sins. Paul said that in the preceding several verses (5:6–11), and now he begins to show how our sins are causal of Christ's death. The why of Christ's death now takes center stage in the Gospel Paul is proclaiming.

"It's a beautiful story," we in the audience might be saying, "but how do I fit into it?" Paul delays just a bit longer in the delivery of the goods, but it is worth it!

The "Wherefore" at the beginning of this section (vv. 12–21) doesn't tie to a single thing in the preceding verses! That's because Paul wants us to return all the way to the beginning; he wants us to review everything that has happened in our drama. Then he will bring us back to the present scene to see that all will be resolved in Jesus Christ.

At this point in his commentary on Romans, Clarke describes a certain Dr. John Taylor of Norwich as "a divine who yielded to few in command of temper, benevolent feeling, and deep acquaintance with the Hebrew and Greek Scriptures, [who]...undertook the elucidation of this much-controverted epistle":

As to the order of time: the apostle carries his arguments backwards from the time when Christ came into the world (chap. 1:17 to chap. 4) to the time when the covenant was made with Abraham (chap. 4), to the time when the judgment to condemnation, pronounced upon Adam, came upon all men, chap.5:12, to the end. And thus he gives us a view of the principal dispensations from the beginning of the world.[21]

Paul himself sums up the whole story in the next ten verses (vv. 12–21) with the addition that now the story has an end: victory in Jesus Christ! Up until now, we were all somewhere "back there," struggling to get out of the world of sin.

The summary in vv. 12 through 14 doesn't add a whole lot to what Paul already has covered in Romans. What impresses us is he can cover, in three verses, everything that happened from 1:18–3:20. We sense that something significant is about to happen. The Gospel account of our history, summarized here in verses 12–14, is comprised in this simple equation: those before the law (from Adam to Moses) have sinned, those after the law have sinned, death entered through sin, and so, therefore, death has reigned up until now. Yes, but we're forgetting the manifestation (the announcement): "But now the righteousness of God without the law is manifested...unto all and upon all them that believe...for all have sinned and come short of the glory of God, being justified freely by his grace through the redemption that is in Christ Jesus" (3:21–24). But before Paul reveals how this justification is accomplished, he sets us up just a little further for his big revelation in the book of Romans.

Before the big revelation in which Paul finally comes forth with the "how" of righteousness and life from grace, he gives us an estimation (as well as his own appreciation) of the superabundance of grace proceeding from God. Our narrator, aware of what's in store for us, has almost been overcome by his own emotions.

"The grace of God more than undid what Adam did," Paul, our narrator, proclaims.

"You decide whether condemnation or grace reveals God's intention from the beginning," Paul says. "For if through the offence of one many be dead, much more the grace of God, and the gift by the grace…hath abounded unto many…for the judgment was by one to condemnation, but the free gift is of many offences unto justification…for if by one man's offence death reigned by one, much more they which receive abundance of grace and of the gift of righteousness shall reign in life by one, Jesus Christ" (vv. 15–17). With this, Paul elevates our expectations of the promise of grace: righteousness and life!

"And now," our narrator can no longer contain his emotions, "without further delay: how God gives righteousness and life from grace!"

18 Therefore as by the offence of one, judgment came upon all men to condemnation; even so by the righteousness of one the free gift came upon all men unto justification of life.

19 For as by one man's disobedience many were made sinners, so by the obedience of one shall many be made righteous.

20 Moreover the law entered, that the offence might abound. But where sin abounded, grace did much more abound:

21 That as sin hath reigned unto death, even so might grace reign through righteousness unto eternal life by Jesus Christ our Lord.

Indigenously, an intense silence has gripped the audience. None of us is looking to the side; nobody is whispering. We've even stopped blinking our eyes! Dramatic images rush to our consciousness: the generations of failure; the narrator shaking his head and saying, "All have sinned!"; the huge, red cross; and the projection screen headline: "That he might be just, and the justifier" (3:25).

Nothing is more settling than understanding, and the feeling among all of us in the audience is the same: "Now I see: Jesus died for *me*. Because God is righteous, and because He is just, the only way God could justify a sinner would be through the payment from an otherwise innocent sin bearer—'by the righteousness of one' (v. 18)."

"Does that refer to Jesus on the cross?" we ask ourselves. "No, wait a minute. The narrator said, 'Through the obedience of the One the many will be made righteous' (v. 19). That implies more.

'That He might be just and the justifier' (3:25)—Jesus Christ obeyed the entire time, His entire life! He is the end of the law (Rom. 10:4), the complete and perfect fulfillment of it. He kept the law perfectly!

"But how is 'the free gift came upon all men' (v. 18) to be understood?" we wonder. There is sufficient agreement of thought in the audience to cause several people to look around and nod their heads at the others. The general feeling is "I like what I have heard, and I hope there's more."

Verses 18 through 21 of chapter 5 deal with Christ's work in man's justification—a "work" that satisfies God's requirements. The key phrases are "the righteousness of one" (v. 18), "by the obedience of one" (v. 19), and "even so might grace reign through righteousness unto eternal life" (v. 21). These three requirements are satisfied in God's mind "by Jesus Christ our Lord" (v. 21).

Consider this: In order for God to be both just and Justifier (3:25), He removes the condemnation of the sinner (because all have "broken the law"—1:18–3:20; 5:12–13), while at the same time, He maintains His own righteousness. But that can't be—because justice (or righteousness) demands that the guilty be punished. Yet if a person who was perfectly just—that is, with no guilt of his own—satisfied this demand and was punished in the sinner's stead, the sinner could go free. Still, this doesn't completely satisfy us because there is still that nagging uneasiness about letting the sinner go free. Would there be some way we could acquire the righteousness of this otherwise innocent sin bearer by somehow sharing in his debt payment experience?

In chapter 5, Paul's use of verb tenses gives a marked completeness to Christ's work in man's salvation. In verse 9 he says, "Being now justified [by his blood], we shall be saved." Again, in verse 10, he writes, "We were reconciled to God [by the death of his Son]…we shall be saved [by his life]." And, finally, in verse 11, he adds, "We have now received the atonement." Jesus worked (in the past) for us by His death, and He will work (in the future) for us by His life!

In the set-up for his discussion of Christ's work in chapter 5, Paul said (referring to Christ), "Who was delivered for our offences, and was raised again for our justification" (4:25). The hope Paul guaranteed to us (5:2–5) is founded on the pardon of the past and the justification of the future—everything falls on Christ! And all of the work He does (and did) satisfies God's justness! The great revelation in this story to the Romans is that Jesus Christ lives to justify and give life. Verses 18 and 19 equally proclaim this. God gives Christ's righteousness (v. 18)—or obedience (v. 19)—to man from God's grace!

Notice at the end of five chapters how on track (and rich!) Paul's five-verse opening to his epistle really is: "Paul...separated unto the gospel of God...concerning his Son Jesus Christ...declared to be the Son of God with power...by the resurrection from the dead: By whom we have received grace" (Rom. 1:1–5).

Maclaren also captures the apostle's wonderful completeness and organization:

> And now, if you will take...this letter, and read over its first eight chapters, what is the apostle talking about when he in them fulfils his purpose and preaches "the Gospel to them that are at Rome also"? Here is, in the briefest possible words, his summary—the universality of sin, the awful burden of guilt, the tremendous outlook of penalty, the impossibility of man rescuing himself or living righteously, the incarnation, and life, and death of Jesus Christ as a sacrifice for the sins of the world, the hand of faith grasping the offered blessing, the indwelling in believing souls of the Divine Spirit, and the consequent admission of man into a life of sonship, power, peace, victory, glory, the child's place in the love of the Father from which nothing can separate. These are the teachings which make the staple of this epistle.[22]

The significance of the first part of verse 20 is that "the law entered in order to show the condition of the sinner to be completely without hope."

"Ahhh," says Paul, "but where sin abounded, grace did much more abound—that as sin hath reigned unto death, even so might grace reign through righteousness unto eternal life by Jesus Christ our Lord" (vv. 20–21). The reign of grace through righteousness is what Paul will take up in chapter 6. In the same manner that Paul conducted us from faith (in Abraham) to grace (in Christ), he will conduct us to the reign of grace in the Romans!

And about the matter of man's part in his justification and of his going free? Look, Paul is telling this story! And we haven't heard yet from the Romans. But the story is all here, and so far, Paul has been a good narrator. Let us witness the final scene!

CHAPTER 5

That Grace Might Continue (6:1–23)

THE RISE OF the curtain reveals a group of some twenty to twenty-five people (men and women) arranged in the form of an irregular circle. Their median age strikes us as being forty to fifty years. Some are sitting on benches, while others are more or less leaning on trees. The scene conveys the image of a town square. The people's attire is loose—a sort of robe (or gown even) with a tie at the waist. The majority of these gowns are pale in color. We don't notice much variety in their dress, and the women don't seem to be dressed much differently from the men. At the center of the circle we spot a single man, of the same attire, who is holding what looks like a scroll.

The impression we get from the chitchat among the people is that they know each other. Before long, a few of them begin nodding their heads, while others point in the direction of the man in the center. The visiting among them stops, and the center man clears his throat. Using both hands, he unrolls what he has been holding at his side, extends his arms (holding the scroll unraveled), glances at his friends in the circle, and opens his mouth to speak. His listeners lean forward, anticipating the reading. The passers-by cast a glance in their direction and, as though they are accustomed to such gatherings, go on past the square. The reader nods, readjusts his scroll, and begins.

"What shall we say then? Shall we continue in sin, that grace may abound?"

Paul's question gives the impression he is speaking face-to-face with the Romans, and it illustrates the distinctive teaching style of Romans. Clarke explains:

> He was a great genius and a fine writer; and he seems to have exercised all his talents, as well as the most perfect Christian temper, in drawing up this epistle. The plan of it is very extensive; and it is surprising to see what a spacious field of knowledge he has comprised, and how many various designs, arguments, explications, instructions, and exhortations, he has executed in so small a compass.[23]

No other New Testament book teaches like Romans! Its distinction is due to the fact that it is the only letter Paul wrote before he had been with its recipients (1:13; 15:22–24). He wanted them to have the whole story—to have the Gospel—as Clarke supports:

> Paul had never been at Rome when he wrote this letter, and therefore it cannot turn upon some particular points, to revive the remembrance of what he had more largely taught in person, or to satisfy the scrupulous in some things he might have touched upon at all; but in it we may expect a full account of his Gospel, or those glad tidings of salvation which he preached among the Gentiles, seeing this epistle was intended to supply the total want of his preaching at Rome.[24]

There is no scarcity of Bible students who have been enthralled by this epistle's magnitude. In the reconstruction of the scenario that could have made up the dispatching of Romans (by Phoebe, included in Paul's salutation in chapter 16), notice the consummate importance James Hastings places on the epistle:

> While that roll of manuscript which Paul gave to Phoebe was the epistle written from Corinth to the Church which was in Rome, an epistle of such consummate importance to the future of Christianity that Renan is hardly exaggerating when he makes the startling statement that Phoebe, as she sailed away from Corinth, "carried beneath the folds of her robe the whole future of Christian theology."[25]

Nor is there any want of readers who recognize the writing genius in the apostle. Notice what Macknight has to say:

> Upon the whole, I heartily agree with Beza in the account which he hath given of the apostle Paul as a writer, 2 Cor. 10:6, note, where he says, "When I more narrowly consider the whole genius and character of Paul's style, I must confess that I have found no such sublimity of speaking in Plato himself, as often as the apostle is pleased to thunder out the mysteries of God; no exquisiteness of vehemence in Demosthenes equal to his, as often as he had a mind either to terrify men with a dread of the divine judgments, or to admonish them concerning their conduct, or to allure them to the contemplation of the divine benignity, or to excite them to the duties of piety and morality. In a word, not even in Aristotle himself, nor in Galen, though most excellent artists, do I find a more exact method of teaching."[26]

The way chapters and verses are arranged in our commonly used Bible versions impairs us somewhat in seeing this. There is no change in subject from chapter 5 to chapter 6. God's grace is what Paul discussed in chapter 5 and what he continues to discuss in chapter 6. And the letter our orator in the square has before him is a letter indeed—without any divisions or interruptions. In any event, the reign of grace "through righteousness unto eternal life by Jesus Christ our Lord" (Rom. 5:21) will set Paul's dissertation course through the end of chapter 6. Paul will transport grace from the rational mind of God in heaven to the earth—and the rational mind of the Romans!

Remain Dead! (6:1–11)

1 What shall we say then? Shall we continue in sin, that grace may abound?

2 God forbid. How shall we, that are dead to sin, live any longer therein?

3 Know ye not, that so many of us as were baptized into Jesus Christ were baptized into his death?

4 Therefore we are buried with him by baptism into death; that like as Christ was raised up from the dead by the glory of the Father even so we also should walk in newness of life.

5 For if we have been planted together in the likeness of his death, we shall be also in the likeness of his resurrection;

6 Knowing this, that our old man is crucified with him, that the body of sin might be destroyed, that henceforth we should not serve sin.

7 For he that is dead is freed from sin.

The only thing to which we can attribute the diverse and unexpected ways in which the Gospel came to us is God's wisdom. Paul's answer to his own question almost by happenstance will complete for us what was lacking in his Gospel. Without the question he asks, we also would be lacking the remainder of the Romans' story (which is revealed in the remainder of chapter 6).

The newness of life for the Romans (v. 4) started with their burial with Christ into death by baptism (vv. 3–4). Christ died, and the Romans by baptism "died" with Him. This "death" was a death to sin. Verse 6 is key here: "Our old man is crucified with him, that the body of sin might be destroyed that henceforth we should not serve sin." The sense of this last phrase is not so much that we should not serve sin—that is, as an exhortation *not* to serve it—but rather, it is a declaration that the Romans' "death" had already freed them *from* sin: "That we should not serve sin."

Two things justify this second rendition: the immediate context and the larger context. The "for" at the beginning of the very next verse (v. 7) has to refer back to the statement of verse 6, and the "for" (v. 7) says, "He that is dead is freed from sin" (that is, liberated, as explained in verse 6). The two verses say the same thing.

The larger context supports this understanding: "Therefore as by the offence of one, judgment came upon all men to condemnation; even so by the righteousness of one the free gift came upon all men unto justification of life" (5:18). Christ's work—that is, His death on the cross and His life of obedience (5:19)—enters into man by baptism to justify him and give him life—all from grace! How do we know Christ does this? By faith, because of what is written (Rom. 4:3, 17, 23–25)! Justification by faith and from grace is no new thing (Abraham proved it!). But baptism into Jesus Christ is new. It is a part of God's righteousness "manifested…at this time" (3:21, 25).

Baptism was how the Romans started their spiritual life and how they received newness of life. It was baptism into Jesus Christ—two people in one single body, with Jesus living to justify and give life from grace.

Our reader in the square uses so much emotion exulting over their liberation from sin that we forget about the question he made at the beginning: "Shall we continue in sin, that grace may abound?" (v. 1). He now pauses a few seconds, checks the listeners, and then returns with intensity.

> 8 Now if we be dead with Christ, we believe that we shall also live with him:
>
> 9 Knowing that Christ being raised from the dead dieth no more; death hath no more dominion over him.
>
> 10 For in that he died, he died unto sin once: but in that he liveth, he liveth unto God.
>
> 11 Likewise reckon ye also yourselves to be dead indeed unto sin, but alive unto God through Jesus Christ our Lord.

Verse 8 constitutes obedience of faith (or by faith—1:5): "Now, if we be dead with Christ, we believe that we shall also live with him." Man does his part (that is, he obeys by dying with Christ) and then trusts that God will do His part. Man trusts that he has newness of life from God. It is in this death with Christ that all of Christ's redeeming, reconciling work leaves heaven and joins itself with man. The Romans had this historical point of entry, this beginning.

Verses 9 and 10 (if we think about them for a minute) fill us with wonder: Jesus Christ resurrected to a different life, a life in God's presence ("He liveth unto God"—v. 10). In his reference to the Romans' baptism, Paul said in verse 4: "Therefore we are buried with him by baptism into death: that like as Christ was raised up from the dead by the glory of the Father, even so we also should walk in newness of life." At baptism, there is a bit of the eternal that is placed in man—a taste of deity!

Verse 11 is the first true exhortation in this section (vv. 1–11). The preceding ten verses have all dealt with past experiences—theirs and Christ's. "All this has already been established previously," is what Paul is saying in verses 1 through 10. But in verse 11, he turns and exhorts them: "Just as Jesus ceased to be alive to sin, you do so," is the significance of that verse. "Continue to treat sin just like you did the instant in which you were being baptized," Paul essentially says, "as though you were dead to sin, and alive to God through Jesus Christ our Lord!"

Now Yield Your Members Servants to Righteousness (6:12–23)

12 Let not sin therefore reign in you mortal body, that ye should obey it in the lusts thereof.

13 Neither yield ye your members as instruments of unrighteousness unto sin: but yield yourselves unto God, as those that are alive from the dead, and your members as instruments of righteousness unto God.

14 For sin shall not have dominion over you: for ye are not under the law, but under grace.

Paul continues to exhort his "fellow saints" (Rom. 1:7) to die to sin—but with a noticeable change of demeanor. The exhortation that extends to the end of our study reveals the gratitude the apostle felt toward God's grace.

He projects this constraint toward his friends in Rome with such expressions as "yield yourselves," "God be thanked," and "obeyed from the heart." More than an exhortation, the remainder of chapter 6 makes up an entreaty constrained by God's mercy and goodness. But the apostle also has reserved for us one or two surprises—a type of revelation—toward the end of the chapter. We still have a couple of lingering questions about man's part in his justification, and the rest of the story of the Romans!

"Let not sin therefore reign"—Paul places man's will at the control center of the reign of grace. Once Paul settles the question of liberation from sin's hold (vv. 1–11), he enters directly into the Romans' lives with a challenging newness of thinking: "Neither yield ye your members as instruments of unrighteousness...but yield yourselves unto God, as those that are alive from the dead." Elkins explains:

> We must not forget that although Romans 6 enables us to instruct more perfectly in the way of the Lord those who are confused concerning baptism, Romans 6 was written to Christians and not to the world. Christians must keep in mind the change of state which they underwent, when they became Christians, and not go back into a life of sin.[27]

"God is going to continue—with your cooperation—His work of grace in you," is what Paul is saying to each Roman saint. Do you recall the good man's desire to do good (2:1–11)? Now—in Christ—the desire to do good counts: "For ye are not under the law, but under grace" (v. 14).

Likewise, do you recall the projection screen announcement: "But now the righteousness of God without the law is manifested...which is by faith of Jesus Christ...being justified freely by his grace" (3:21–24)? In Christ we have much more, don't we?

15 What then? Shall we sin, because we are not under the law, but under grace? God forbid.

16 Know ye not, that to whom ye yield yourselves servants to obey, his servants ye are to whom ye obey; whether of sin unto death, or of obedience unto righteousness?

17 But God be thanked, that ye were the servants of sin, but ye have obeyed from the heart that form of doctrine which was delivered you.

18 Being then made free from sin, ye became the servants of righteousness.

Liberation from law and liberation from sin: two things God's grace gives us through righteousness (5:20–21). The Gospel's whole objective is to give us God's righteousness (1:16–17) without the law. And we can receive this righteousness through faith in Christ: "Therefore as by the offence of one, judgment came upon all men to condemnation, even so by the righteousness of one the free gift came upon all men unto justification of life. For as by one man's disobedience many were made sinners, so by the obedience of one shall many by made righteous" (5:18–19).

In the answer Paul gives to his question—"Shall we sin because we are not under the law, but under grace?" (v. 15)—he refers to an acknowledgment in the Romans that without the question we would be unaware of: that by being baptized they had declared they wanted what God was offering them—righteousness: "Ye have obeyed from the heart" (v. 17).

"Death to sin" (Rom. 6:2) is simply a different way of expressing this desire to do good. The form of doctrine (v. 17) is this "death to the old/life to the new" concept, expressed in baptism (Rom. 6:4). The proof of this is that the result in each instance is the same: compare verse 18 ("being then made free from sin") to verse 4 ("even so we also should walk in newness of life").

The two questions in verses 1 and 15 lead to—and the two answers refer to—the same historical point in the Romans' lives: the point of submission to this "death to the old/life to the new" teaching—the point of their baptism! But why does Paul give so much attention to that Roman beginning? Because they needed to continue in that submission to make the grace continue. "Remember," Paul is saying, "ye became the servants of righteousness" (v. 18). In the appeal that follows (vv. 19-23), Paul ramifies toward eternity the implications of this "old-to-new" thinking for everyone.

> 19 I speak after the manner of men because of the infirmity of your flesh: for as ye have yielded your members servants to uncleanness and to iniquity unto iniquity; even so now yield your members servants to righteousness unto holiness.
>
> 20 For when ye were the servants of sin, ye were free from righteousness.
>
> 21 What fruit had ye then in those things whereof ye are now ashamed?
>
> 22 But now being made free from sin, and become servants to God, ye have your fruit unto holiness, and the end everlasting life.

"I speak after the manner of men because of the infirmity of your flesh"—we can see our public reader pause, take several steps in the direction of his friends in front of him, and then begin a deliberate stroll, following the inside formation of the circle. As he reads, he occasionally glances at his listeners, and then continues to read, walking along.

"As ye have yielded your members servants to uncleanness and to iniquity unto iniquity." With scarcely more than a few pen strokes, the apostle has transported the Romans (and us) the entire way back to the world from where they had come: the world of sin. Scenes of disorder come to our minds: revels, fits of rage, drunkenness.

"Even so now yield your members servants to righteousness"—the reader emphasizes his lines, projecting the apostle Paul's feeling—"unto holiness!"

He pauses to check their response.

The call to be of Jesus (1:6–7) is a call (or an appeal) to renounce our service-commitment to the world of sin and to voluntarily do service to the things of God. It is a process—one that starts with baptism into Jesus Christ and then continues for the rest of our lives. Paul told us that "the law entered, that the offence might abound" (5:20). "But where sin abounded, grace did much more abound, that as sin hath reigned unto death, even so might grace reign through righteousness unto eternal life by Jesus Christ our Lord" (5:20–21). The grace will continue to reign, provided righteousness continues to reign. But the desire for good counts—by Jesus Christ our Lord! It is this desire to do good that constitutes death to sin.

Holiness comes from the Greek *hagios*, which means "set apart or separated." The Romans had been "called of Jesus Christ; called to be saints" (or "holy ones"—1:6–7). They had been—by the Gospel—"separated" from the world of sin. And this separation was to continue. By their death with Jesus Christ, each one of them was made holy (by attributed righteousness). Through their life with Jesus they were to continue to be made holy by the process of "holiness-ing" (elsewhere rendered "sanctification"). And this does indeed—along with *Christ's* work —involve work on the part of *man*!

"But why put out all this effort?" we might ask. In which case Paul would respond, "We...rejoice in hope of

71

the glory of God" (5:1–2)! The Gospel essentially is the history— related by God—of the restoration of glory. And God's history makes itself credible by its fusion with *our* history—a fusion that reveals God's glory by displaying it in His Son (1:1–4). But the chasm is wide, and the withdrawing has been going on for a long time. It's going to take a lot of holiness-ing!

Our stage-square orator has completed his inner-circle stroll. Meditating, he returns to his place at the center, nodding as he goes. He extends his arms with his palms facing up and lifts his shoulders, while at the same time pulling them in. (He is trying to convey the apostle's sentiment.)

He begins, "For when ye were the servants of sin, ye were free from righteousness."

The picture of the Gentiles—the irreverent ones—comes to mind.

Through Paul, we are given the Romans' history "back when." What comes to mind in this instance isn't the Jews. The unending list of the Gentiles' bad traits (1:18–32) is what Paul's words call up. Remember, the irreverent type didn't even care—they had already thrown themselves into the party. The Gentiles hadn't seen any profit whatsoever in serving righteousness. And now, here they are, "dead to sin"—if they listen to Paul!

The orator continues, raising his voice a bit. "What fruit had ye then…?" The city-square orator, seeing he is nearing a conclusion, begins to speak more deliberately, emphasizing certain words for attention. "In those things whereof ye are now ashamed?…For the end of those things is death!"

His countenance here is striking, but we sense that his listeners know he is on their side.

The speaker relents a bit, dons a smile, and then returns with boldness. "But now, being made free from sin, and become servants to God, ye have your fruit unto holiness!… And the end —." The speaker pauses, catches his breath, and when he is certain all are attentive, adds, "everlasting life!"

In the audience, we have forgotten about the listeners in the circle, so captivated have we been by the words of the speaker. Without realizing it, we have slipped all the way out to the edges of our seats. When, due to the sudden halt in the oratory, we come to, we again remember the people in the circle. Like us, they have been left dumbfounded by the delivery. Some of them are resting a chin on a hand, while others simply stare straight ahead, lost in their thoughts. Several sigh and then nod at each other in a type of communication. The impression we get is that their feeling is the same as ours: "We have heard what we needed to hear."

"For," so enthralled are we by the somberness of the moment that the speaker's interruption strikes us as irreverent, "the wages of sin is death!…But the gift of God is eternal life through Jesus Christ our Lord!"

"Sin…death…gift of God…life …through Jesus Christ."

It's as if a light bulb has just come on! In a single instant, all the parts of the drama simultaneously converge on a single point of destination: "through Jesus Christ."

Baptized "into Jesus Christ" (6:3).

Dead unto sin "through Jesus Christ" (6:11).

Life "through Jesus Christ" (6:23).

"Ohhh," we say. "Now I see. 'The redemption that is in Christ Jesus; whom God hath set forth to be a propitiation through faith in his blood…the free gift came upon all men.'"

We have to die with Him.

Then His experience becomes ours.

Everything of His becomes ours "through Jesus Christ."

All have sinned, all have died. The free gift came upon all men by Jesus' righteousness (Rom. 6:23).

> Therefore as by the offence of one judgment came upon all men to condemnation; even so by the righteousness of one the free gift came upon all men unto justification of life.
>
> —Romans 5:18

> That as sin hath reigned unto death, even so might grace reign through righteousness unto eternal life by Jesus Christ our Lord.
>
> —Romans 5:21

And the curtain drops.

Glossary

Baptized: Comes from the Greek *baptidzo*, meaning "to immerse." The Romans were immersed into Jesus Christ: His life and His death (6:3). The identification with Christ's experience—"buried [with Him] into death"—is too vivid to refer to belief alone. The physical act of immersion in water—and thus appropriating Christ's work by faith—is what gave the Romans "newness of life" (6:4).

Newness of life: The holiness God gives by justifying through faith in Christ. The same spirit of holiness that declares Jesus Christ to be "Son of God"(1:3–4), declares those baptized into Christ to be "holy ones" (saints—1:7). Life, then, begins anew.

Endnotes

1. Joseph Henry Thayer, D.D., *A Greek-English Lexicon of the New Testament,* Baker Book House, Grand Rapids, Michigan, 1979, p. 68.

2. Merrill C. Tenney, *The Zondervan Pictorial Bible Dictionary,* Zondervan Publishing House, Grand Rapids, Michigan, 1981, p. 318.

3. Harold K. Moulton, *The Analytical Greek Lexicon Revised,* Zondervan Publishing House, Grand Rapids, Michigan, 1979, p. 433.

4. Thayer, *Op. Cit.,* p. 511.

5. W.J. Conybeare, M.A., & J.S. Howson, D.D., *The Life and Epistles of St. Paul,* Wm. B. Eerdmans Publishing Company, Grand Rapids, Michigan, 1957, p. 508.

6. Adam Clarke, L.L.D., F.S.A., *Clarke's Commentary, Volume VI, Romans – Revelation,* Abingdon Press, New York, Nashville, 1832, p. 37.

7. Joseph S. Exell, *The Biblical Illustrator, Romans—Vol. I,* Baker Book House, Grand Rapids, Michigan, p. 25.

8. *Ibid.*, p. 25.

9. *Ibid.*, pp. 27–28.

10. Tenney, *Op. Cit.* (*Epistle To The Romans*, James Oliver Buswell, Jr.), p. 730.

11. *Ibid.*, p. 730.

12. James Macknight, D.D., *A New Literal Translation, from the Original Greek of All the Apostolical Epistles*, Gospel Advocate Company, Nashville, 1954, p. 58.

13. Clarke, *Op. Cit.*, p. 42.

14. Clarke, *Op. Cit.*, p. 42.

15. Garland Elkins and Thomas B. Warren, *The Living Messages of the Books of the New Testament*, National Press, Jonesboro, Arkansas, p. 107.

16. Clarke, *Op. Cit.*, p. 40.

17. Elkins, *Op. Cit.*, pp. 111–112.

18. Clarke, *Op. Cit.*, p. 65.

19. Elkins, *Op. Cit.*, p. 105.

20. Alexander Maclaren, D.D., Litt. D, *Expositions of Holy Scripture—Romans—*Grand Rapids, Michigan, 1978, p. 87.

21. Clarke, *Op. Cit.*, pp. 6, 70.

22. Maclaren, *Op. Cit.*, pp. 33–34.

23. Clarke, *Op. Cit.*, p. 31.

24. Clarke, *Op. Cit.*, p. 31.

25. James Hastings, *The Great Texts of the Bible: Acts – Romans I–VIII*, Wm. B. Eerdmans Publishing Company, Grand Rapids, Michigan, p. 237.

26. Macknight, *Op. Cit.*, p. 26.

27. Elkins, *Op. Cit.*, p. 102.

Bibliography

Clarke, Adam, *Clarke's Commentary, Volume VI, Romans – Revelation*, Abingdon Press, New York, Nashville, 1832.

Conybeare, M. A., and Howson, D. D., *The Life and Epistles of St. Paul*, Wm. B. Eerdmans Publishing Company, Grand Rapids, Michigan, 1957.

Elkins, Garland, and Warren, Thomas B., *The Living Messages of the Books of the New Testament,* National Press, Jonesboro, Arkansas.

Exell, Joseph S., *The Biblical Illustrator, Romans—Vol. I,* Baker Book House, Grand Rapids, Michigan.

Hastings, James, *The Great Texts of the Bible: Acts – Romans I–VIII*, Wm. B. Eerdmans Publishing Company, Grand Rapids, Michigan.

Macknight, James, *A New Literal Translation from the Original Greek of All the Apostolical Epistles*, Gospel Advocate Company, Nashville, 1954.

Maclaren, Alexander, *Expositions of Holy Scripture—Romans*, Grand Rapids, Michigan, 1978.

Moulton, Harold K., *The Analytical Greek Lexicon Revised*, Zondervan Publishing House, Grand Rapids, Michigan, 1979.

Tenney, Merrill C., *The Zondervan Pictorial Bible Dictionary*, Zondervan Publishing House, Grand Rapids, Michigan, 1981.

Thayer, Joseph Henry, *A Greek-English Lexicon of the New Testament*, Baker Book House, Grand Rapids, Michigan, 1979.

About the Author

*J*ERRY SERIGHT IS a preacher, missionary, and son of missionaries. From ages one to seventeen, he traveled with his parents as they ministered in the Brazilian states of Pernambuco, Piaui, and Minas Gerais, giving him a profound knowledge of both the Portuguese language and Brazilian culture. In 2001, he returned to northeast Brazil, where he worked with fellow members of the Church of Christ in Salvador and Aracaju, before returning home to Lubbock, Texas.

Seright holds a preacher-training certificate from the Sunset International Bible Institute and a bachelor of arts degree, with an emphasis in Bible, from Lubbock Christian University. He has four years' experience in preaching, as well as many years in Bible teaching to various age groups. Additionally, he has written articles in church bulletins and Christian newspapers, and he is chronicling development in the Churches of Christ from 1975—the year he was baptized—to present.

Seright currently resides in Irving, Texas, where he is actively involved in preaching and teaching at the South Macarthur Church of Christ. He fondly remembers his Brazilian experience and eagerly awaits an opportunity to return to Brazil. Seright's two adult sons and daughters have followed with interest the production of the present work. Curtis, his younger son, was with him in Brazil when the original manuscript was written in Portuguese, and Christopher, his elder son, produced the opening page layout. Additionally, Catherine and Carrie, his daughters, lent encouragement and also input advice on chapter-opening layout.

Breinigsville, PA USA
10 September 2009
223806BV00001B/15/P